D0401930

# Also by Daniel Brand

# The Irishman:

*Frank Sheeran's True Crime Story*

thought of as universal. As befitting its nature, it is presented without assurance regarding its prolonged validity or interim quality. Trademarks that are mentioned are done without written consent and can in no way be considered an endorsement from the trademark holder.

# Introduction

FRANK SHEERAN, KNOWN as the Irishman, waited his entire life to tell his story—or at least, his version of his story. The world knew him as a union official, a long-time member of the Teamsters Union, and a member of Jimmy Hoffa's inner circle at the top of the national union. He had run-ins with the law in this position. He was charged with the murder of a rebel union member in a riot that occurred outside the Teamster's Local Philadelphia Union Hall, but the charges were later dropped. He went to prison in the 80s after being caught on a wire instructing one of his crew to break someone's legs and was named in Rudy Giuliani's Mafia Commission Trial as an unindicted co-conspirator and one of only two non-Italian members of the Mafia Commission.

As an old man suffering from cancer that would soon kill him, Frank Sheeran shared his story with his attorney. He told him of the things that were already known—his work with the Teamsters, friendship with Hoffa, and his connections to the mob. That turned out to be the tip of the iceberg. Sheeran talked about his years in the Army, serving in Europe during the second world war. He detailed the war crimes he committed—killing German and Italian POWs. He provided more information about his work for the mafia, admitting to several mob hits he performed for his friend Russell Bufalino, the head of the Northeastern Pennsylvania Mafia family.

More shockingly, he admitted to involvement or connection to other, high profile, mafia-related crimes such as providing weapons for the Bay of Pigs Invasion and maybe even the assassination of President Kennedy and the brazen murder of "Mafioso Crazy" Joe Gallo. Of all of the shocking revelations, he admitted to the murder of Jimmy Hoffa, a man he had worked with and had formed a friendship with for over 20 years.

The truths of his confession have not yet been verified, and, for some of his claims, there are conflicting accounts and facts. That said, it is a story worth being considered, as it provides insight into the often shadowy world of organized crime, at least as it was in the recent past.

# Chapter 1: Sheeran's WWII Years and First Murders

APRIL 29, 1945

The men of the 3rd Battalion, 157th Infantry Regiment of the 45th Infantry Division under the command of Lieutenant Colonel Felix L. Sparks, slowly made their way towards the Dachau concentration camp near Munich in the German state of Bavaria. Among them was a 24-year-old private by the name of Frank Sheeran. Hailing from the working-class neighborhoods of Darby Pennsylvania, just outside of Philadelphia, Sheeran was a large man—barrel-chested and standing at six foot four. The things his unit would find a Dachau would haunt his dreams for the rest of his life.

Dachau was the first concentration camp opened in Germany under the Nazi regime. Its doors opened in 1933, soon after Hitler came into power in Berlin. It was situated just outside Munich, the city where Hitler's first attempt to seize power, the Beer Hall Putsch in 1923, both started and ended. Unlike some of the later camps like Auschwitz, where Jews and other groups that the Nazis considered undesirable were systematically put to death, Dachau was mainly used initially for German political prisoners, though by the end, its overcrowded barracks and subcamps housed prisoners of all kinds.

While not a death camp, death was a constant companion of its many prisoners. Hundreds were murdered, while others were subjected to medical experiments on the effects and treatment of hypothermia. Prisoners were forced into ice-cold baths until hypothermia set in and then 'treated' in a variety of different methods from scalding baths to even forcing female prisoners to be intimate with them. Other experiments included subjecting prisoners to different air pressures to study the effects of the bends.

By April of 1945, the Germans knew they were losing the war, and the Nazis in charge knew there was little hope. The Red Army of the Soviet Union had taken Poland and moved closer to Berlin every day. To the west and south, the Allies, led by Great Britain and the United States, had liberated France and toppled the Nazi puppet regime of Benito Mussolini and his National Fascist Party in Italy. They had pushed back after the Germans undertook their final offensive in the Battle of the Bulge and finally entered German territory as they started to take the Western cities on their way towards Berlin slowly. On the 29th of April, Hitler was deep in his bunker, watching his thousand-year Reich crumble after less than 20 years. He would kill himself a little after three in the afternoon the next day.

The SS, or Schutzstaffel translating to "Protection Squadron" in English, which was left in charge of the concentration camps, began to plan for what would happen at the end of the war. They had orders to kill the prisoners. Some were to be shipped north to the Baltic sea where they would be drowned, while others were to be taken south into the Alps, where they would be used as slave labor by resisting SS members after Nazi Germany fell.

They did not have much of a chance to put this plan into action before the Americans came. Thousands of prisoners were forced into a death march soon before the Americans arrived, and those to be sent to the Baltic to be drowned had been put into train cars for the journey. However, the trains never took off, and they were left to die in the train cars. The SS leadership fled and ordered their subordinates to destroy as much evidence of their crimes before surrendering the camp to the Americans.

The Americans that would soon liberate the camp had heard rumors of the atrocities committed by the Nazis in the concentration camps. The Red Army had liberated Auschwitz months earlier—and other camps, such as Majdanek even earlier, but news from the eastern front did not easily travel to the US Soldiers on the ground.

As they approached the camp, they came upon the rail yard first, finding thirty-nine boxcars full of emaciated naked bodies of those that had died of dehydration after the SS had left them in the train cars. Frank Sheeran would never forget the smell of so much death. Some of the US Soldiers began to weep; others could not hold their lunches and vomit at the sight and smell that assaulted them. For most, Frank included, it left them with a profound rage.

Moving closer to the camp itself, they called to the SS in charge of the camp to surrender and received machine-gun fire from a guard tower as a response. Once they had dispatched that pocket of resistance, they entered the camp itself and found even more death. Room after room in the cement structures built in

ie camp was full of the dead and emaciated prisoners stacked
om floor to ceiling, hundreds to a room.

By this time, the 42nd Infantry Division had arrived and ac-
epted the surrender of the current SS commander of the camp,
Heinrich Wicker, who had been left in charge when the top
S officers fled in the days before. Frank Sheeran recalled that
Wicker and a few of the other commanders were ushered into a
ouple of jeeps that drove off. He remembered hearing gunfire
oon after. The bodies of Heinrich Wicker and the other top
commanders were never found.

Some of the other SS in charge of the camp suffered similar
ates. Several were rounded up by US Soldiers near the train yard
where Sheeran and his unit first came upon the bodies of the vic-
ims held in Dachau where they were cut down with machine
gunfire. Other SS guards, those that were the most sadistic towards the prisoners, were killed by the prisoners themselves. A
couple was beaten to death by prisoners when the Americans
first came to the camp, and others were caught trying to flee
dressed as peasants. Sheeran would later claim that he and other
troops would give their guns to the prisoners to let them handle
the killing of the former guards.

The exact amount of SS prisoners of war that were killed in
the Dachau reprisals is unknown to history, but historians now
believe that it was somewhere between thirty and fifty. Sheeran claimed that between the prisoners and the American troops,
somewhere around 500 SS guards and officials lost their lives after the liberation of Dachau and that he killed more than a few
himself. It wasn't the first time Frank Sheeran had killed someone in cold blood, and it certainly wouldn't be the last.

Frank Sheeran signed up as a volunteer for the army in the summer of 1941. He was twenty at the time and had already lived a difficult yet interesting life. He was born in 1920 to an Irish father and Swedish mother, whom he credits for his body size. His mother was taller than his father and never weighed under 200 pounds. Sheeran's father was likely an alcoholic who worked a variety of jobs from being a janitor to a steelworker—building bridges and buildings—but was frequently out of work, leading to the family moving a lot when his father fell behind on rent.

Sheeran's father was also an amateur boxer and taught his son how to fight. He would use these skills at speakeasies. His father would bring him to new speakeasies in the Philadelphia area, where they were not known and goad others into letting their sons box the younger Sheeran and bet on his son winning. Sheeran was also used by his father in the small-time theft of crops among the farms across the bridge in New Jersey. This was Sheeran's first step in his life of crime, and one of his first memories was getting birdshot removed from his behind by his mother after one of these nighttime burglaries was interrupted by a shotgun-wielding farmer.

Early in life, Sheeran developed an aversion to authority that would stay with him his entire life. He frequently played pranks as a schoolboy, once leaving stinky Limburger cheese on the radiator one morning at school, allowing it to melt and stink up the entire classroom. His father would react to these by using Sheeran as a literal punching bag, putting on a pair of boxing gloves, and beating his son for the infraction.

When Sheeran was in 9th grade, the principal at his high school spotted him in the back of the head after another prank.

Sheeran responded with a punch that broke the man's jaw and led to his expulsion. Standing up to his father, Sheeran left home instead of accepting another beating as his punching bag. After a series of odd jobs, Sheeran found a position in a traveling carnival on a tour of New England. This led him to Maine, where he joined a logging company and worked off any remaining fat he had as a member of a two-man saw the team for a couple of years and boxing the other workers in their off time.

Hitching his way back home after that, he spent the next few years working an apprenticeship at a glass company, spending most of his off time chasing girls and taking them dancing six nights a week until he signed up for the army.

Once Sheeran signed up for the service, he was sent to Biloxi, Mississippi, for basic training. Sheeran's issues with authority followed him into the army. He was often defiant in the face of authority and continued to pull pranks when he could. Once, he was given KP duty, peeling potatoes just like in the war movies for giving his drill sergeant lip. He responded by adding laxatives to the coffee but was caught when he was the only person in the unit not spending their day in the latrines.

Even with his aversion to authority, he was initially assigned to the military police. While he had yet to grow into his full six foot four size, at six foot one, he still cut an imposing figure that would make other Soldiers think twice when dealing with him. They shipped him off to the West Coast soon after Pearl Harbor was attacked by the Japanese, as part of the defenders of the West Coast as America joined the war against the Germans and Japanese.

One of the consequences of the Americans' declaration of war was that it gave existing military men a chance to switch positions. When Sheeran was sent to the MPs, he wasn't given a choice, but he took the chance after Pearl Harbor and tried to join the paratroopers. After a disastrous training wherein he jumped off a tower, which left him with a dislocated shoulder, he was scrubbed out of the paratroopers and sent to the infantry.

It took two more years before he saw action. After being sent to Casablanca in 1943 with the 45th Division, his unit was sent to Sicily, where they assisted in taking control of the island in the months after the initial Allied Invasion. The 45th Division had a colorful history prior to Sheeran's inclusion in 1943. General Patton had called it his "Killer Division," and in many of his speeches and orders to them, he had insinuated that they should take no prisoners. They complied with this in many cases, including the Biscari Massacre in Sicily, where dozens of captured Italian and even a couple of German troops were lined up along the runway and cut down with Thompson machine guns. The Soldier responsible then walked the line, shooting any that still moved in the heart.

These sorts of killings in war, while, without a doubt, war crimes in defiance of the Geneva Conventions on the Treatment of Prisoners of War, were not uncommon—and in the heat of war, they were almost "understandable." Seeing friends die at the hands of the enemy can make someone much less likely to accept the surrender of those enemies. Snipers were held in particular derision by those of both sides, as they could kill from so far away, keeping Soldiers on edge at all times. Sheeran was told early when he first went to Sicily that snipers were to be killed when found, never to take one prisoner.

As Sheeran's unit reached Sicily after the initial invasion, he found little combat there. The Italians' hearts were not in the war at this point. After a series of Italian military defeats in North Africa during 1942 and 1943, Benito Mussolini's Fascist government had dismissed him as prime minister, though he had dictatorial control since 1925 and arrested him. The Germans rescued him and put him back in charge of the Italian Social Republic that had nominal control of the northern half of Italy—though this was, in fact, a puppet state that only existed due to German military power, and Mussolini had little control. Once the German Military had been removed from the island, Sheeran found the Sicilians friendly and began his lifelong love of red wine when he drank his fill in Sicily. He would look back fondly on those weeks in the coming months when his unit moved on to the invasion of the Italian mainland.

Sheeran's unit was part of the amphibious landing at Salerno, to the south of Naples, in the Campania region of Italy. Like the more famous D-Day invasion that would occur nine months later, Sheeran's unit—joined by other American units in Sicily at the time as well as British units from Tunisia, Tripoli, and Oran—combined to attack a fortified beach in what was called Operation Avalanche. The ships in the Tyrrhenian Sea shelled the fortified German positions, while Sheeran boarded one of the amphibious landing crafts and made the journey towards the beach.

The plan was to move up the beach one thousand yards and take control of the German position. Under heavy machine-gunning and shelling from the fortified German bunkers and strafing bombing runs by the German Luftwaffe, the Allied forces succeeded in gaining a beachhead. Sheeran's unit were all equipped with shovels that they used to create defensive trenches as more and more American and British troops came to shore.

It was in this battle that Sheeran killed his first man—likely men—but in the chaos of fighting for his life, he couldn't recall the exact details.

Once the Allies had the beachhead, the battle became a stalemate, as the Allies fought to expand their holdings on the beach and waited for the armored divisions and their tanks before pushing further into the German lines. Unfortunately, the Germans used these days to bring their own armored units and artillery into position. The Germans counterattacked, which caused many casualties, but this was pushed back with naval support. The Germans retreated to the more defendable mountains to the south of Rome, leaving Southern Italy to the Allies. All told, over six thousand allied troops were killed or missing after Operation Avalanche succeeded.

With the Germans in retreat, the Allies moved north towards lapels and then into the Apennine mountains as winter was setting in. The Germans had pulled back into the fortified monastery of Monte Cassino, where they could control the land routes into Rome. The Germans in Monte Cassino kept the Allied troops, Sheeran included, pinned down for over 70 days. They had observers strategically stationed so that they could watch all of the allied movements, covering them with artillery and snipers. After multiple failed attacks on the monastery, even after shelling it, Sheeran's unit was among those pulled back to Naples in advance of another naval invasion to the north of Monte Cassino, in Anzio, in an attempt to flank them.

The Allies took the Germans at Anzio by surprise and easily secured a beachhead, taking hundreds of Germans prisoner—but the generals in charge, fearing the ease of taking the beach was part of a trap, declined to push the advantage until armored units and artillery could join them. This was a costly mistake. The Germans regrouped and dug in, with Hitler ordering his troops to remove the beachhead with extreme force. Sheeran soon found his foxhole subjected to almost continuous assault from artillery shells and straining Luftwaffe planes.

This foxhole was Sheeran's home for almost four months of constant shelling and aerial attack. They had covered the top with boards and branches to protect them from the weather and snipers. During daylight, leaving the foxhole was impossible due to the number of snipers watching. The men would relieve themselves in their helmets and empty them outside when night had fallen. They could not start fires, so they ate their rations cold and out of the can, at least when they received more rations as the Germans were also shelling the supply ships when they could.

The night might have given some solace from snipers, but it was also when the Germans could unleash their biggest artillery piece: the railroad gun. Called the Schwerer Gustav by the Germans, it was the largest mobile artillery piece ever used in combat. The Germans had designed it to attack the Maginot Line defenses the French had built along their border with Germany after the First World War. It could shoot a seven-ton shell almost 30 miles. For mobility, they were built onto rail cars so they could be moved by locomotives. In Italy, during the Battle for Anzio, the Germans would move and camouflage it before daylight to keep the Allied shells and bombers from destroying it. Once night fell, they unleashed it, frightening and demoralizing the allied troops. 6,000 more allied troops died in the four months they were dug into the beaches at Anzio.

By this point, the allied troops to the south finally succeeded in taking Monte Cassino from the Germans and were able to join the allied troops like Sheeran, who had been dug into the beaches of Anzio. The Allies pushed north and took Rome without a fight. As in Sicily, when there was little fighting, Sheeran took time to enjoy the city, often drinking wine in the sidewalk cafes. He went AWOL on occasion and in his own words, "had a few adventures." in Rome, though he was never AWOL when his unit had combat, that would have had capital consequences.

After spending almost half a year in Rome and northern Italy, his unit was tasked with a third amphibious landing, this time in southern France. The D-Day invasion of northern France had occurred in the previous month, and the noose on Germany was beginning to tighten. Sheeran's unit came under some fire. Sheeran thought he had been hit when he looked down and discovered himself covered in red liquid. After calling for a medic, he discovered that it was not blood—but wine. His canteen had been shot.

Movement into France was relatively easy. The major invasion was to the north, and the Germans were plotting their final offensive in the Ardennes in what would be known as the Battle of the Bulge. Sheeran and his unit made their way into the Alsace-Lorraine region. This was the contentious area that both France and Germany claimed ownership of and led to several wars between the two powers.

It was here that Sheeran admitted to his first killing of POWs, claiming it was expected. He was given a group of prisoners to take back behind the front lines, but instead of taking them to prisoner of war camps behind the lines, he took them out of sight and shot them. In his words, "I did what I had to do." As his unit moved further into Germany, his extra-legal killings continued and grew. While his unit was patrolling the Harz Mountains, where the Germans had some mountaintop strongholds, they came upon a mule train moving hot meals up to one of those German fortresses. They let the women go, as they were noncombatants, but ate what they wanted of the food before befouling the rest with their bodily fluids. For the German Soldiers, they forced them to dig their own graves before killing them.

Sheeran's unit continued to move further into Germany, with Munich their ultimate goal, passing Nuremberg, the sight of so many of Hitler's biggest rallies—though, by the time they passed through, it had been bombed beyond recognition. This was when they discovered the atrocities at Dachau and where Sheeran killed his last POW. His next illegal kill would be back in the states. Within a few weeks of taking Dachau, the war in Europe ended with Germany's unconditional surrender. Japan would surrender a few months later, and soon after that, Sheeran was discharged. All told, he spent four hundred and eleven days in combat, more than three hundred more than the average American Soldier.

# Chapter 2: Returning Home and The Beginning of Sheeran's Life of Crime

AFTER THE WAR HAD FINISHED, Frank Sheeran, like so many other American Soldiers, found himself discharged and on his way back to the States—in his case, for the first time since he was shipped out to Casablanca in 1943. Coincidentally, Frank bumped into his kid brother Tom while waiting for their ships in October of 1945 in the French port city of Havre de Grace in Normandy, known today simply as Le Havre, the port in English.

Tom had a much different childhood than Frank. While their father would often use Frank as a literal punching bag in response to the scrapes and pranks he got into as a child, Tom had never suffered those types of beatings. Frank Sheeran did not speculate as to the reasons behind this, but it's possible that Tom, seeing the consequences of his older brother's actions, kept his nose clean. Tom had seen some combat—but it was nothing compared to what Frank had been through in the war—and he noticed a difference in Frank both in how he looked and acted compared to prior to the war. He told his brother as much, and deep down, Frank knew he was right. Four hundred and eleven days in combat changes a man.

Having survived the war, Frank Sheeran had a feeling of almost invincibility for surviving something that had cut down so many others. He had experienced more deaths and misery in the last two years than most people go through in their entire lives. He had seen the prisoners who had survived the Nazi concentration camps, almost nothing but skin and bones from prolonged starvation—and he had seen those that didn't survive, stacked like cordwood by the hundreds. He had watched men that he had known as well as 19-year-old kids get cut down by machine-gun fire and bleed out in front of him.

Seeing his younger brother after so many years caused him to wonder how his life would have been different if he hadn't volunteered for combat and if he had remained in the Military Police after Pearl Harbor was bombed. He might have stayed stateside for the entire war, likely dancing six nights a week like he did before he was shipped out. Given the eventual trajectory of his life post-war, it would have differed drastically had he not made that one choice.

When he returned to the states, Frank Sheeran returned to living with his parents, who now had moved into West Philadelphia. The army had given him $100 a month for the first three months after he returned, and like so many other returning American Soldiers, he had difficulty resuming civilian life. A lot can change in a few years, and Sheeran noticed that the men who had stayed home had all of the good jobs. He tried to return to the life he had before the war, even returning to the glassworks and resuming his apprenticeship, but he ended up quitting after only a few months.

Sheeran had always had difficulty with authority and being told what to do. His time in the war had taught him to follow two rules. First, do whatever you could to survive and follow orders in combat. Failing to do either in combat could have deadly consequences, and failure to follow orders could have led to an on-the-spot execution, though the military's rules likely say differently. When it came to following instructions or orders of his civilian bosses after the war, Sheeran just could not be bothered to.

These attitude changes were reinforced by what today would have been diagnosed as Post Traumatic Stress Syndrome or PTSD. Sheeran had constant nightmares about the deaths and horrors he had seen in Europe as well as the things he did there. These would wake him up, and it often took him more than a few minutes to realize he was in a bed in Philadelphia instead of a foxhole on a bomb-cratered beach in Italy. He was not alone in his suffering—nightmares such as this were likely common among some of the men returning from combat duty, but as was common at the time, he suffered in masculine silence and drank.

Having found a taste for it, initially in Sicily but refined in Rome and then the south of France, Frank found himself drinking more and more red wine. A form of self-medication for his undiagnosed PTSD, this became a lifelong issue for him and, at some points, almost killed him. Given that his father was an alcoholic as well, he could have had a genetic predisposition, but as with PTSD, this was not exactly understood in the late 40s.

After he left the glasswork, he moved around from odd job to odd job. He worked construction for a while. He became a delivery person for an ice and coal company, dropping off blocks of ice to keep people's iceboxes cold in the summer and coal to heat their homes in the winter. He spent months working at a cement factory, loading bags of cement into trucks. He even worked part-time as a ballroom dance instructor. His disrespect for authority led to a swift end to many of these jobs. He worked briefly on an assembly line in a blueberry pie factory, but after an altercation with his boss, the man ended up knocked out on the conveyor belt with his mouth stuffed with frozen blueberries. The police had to be called to drag him from the building.

At that point, his mother tried to help and pulled some strings to get him a place in the Pennsylvania State Police as an officer—he only had to pass the physical exam. He was in great shape and would have passed the physical, but he chose not to try. He blamed to have earned everything he got, at least before the war, but his time in combat had changed that. To him, seeing what he had seen during the war, and doing what he did change how he looked at the world. It made him more open to taking. Whether this was a genuine change or the sort of thing a lifelong criminal says looking back on his life in an attempt to justify his previous actions, only Frank Sheeran can know.

Frank Sheeran kept taking odd jobs, finding work where he could, but things started to change after a fateful trip with a few friends. He had piled into a car with some buddies and gone downtown to sell their blood for money to buy more alcohol. After giving blood, they passed a sign for a carnival that offered $100 for anyone who could last three rounds with a boxing kangaroo. Sheeran had been boxing off and on since he was a child. How tough could it be to beat a kangaroo?

The answer, it turned out, was much tougher than expected. Even before Sheeran entered the ring, he became distracted by someone in the audience: Mary Leddy. Sheeran had seen her before he left for the war, but he had never spoken to her. Now, drunk and a bit woozy from giving blood, he found her irresistible and decided to impress her with his kangaroo boxing prowess.

The first round did not go to Sheeran's plans. He started carefully, not wanting to hurt the kangaroo. He gave it a few jabs in the jaw to little effect. The kangaroo would punch back, but Sheeran could take that. Unexpectedly, when he punched the kangaroo, something would slam into the back of his head. Sheeran didn't realize that it was the Kangaroo's tail, which they use as a weapon defensively.

In the second round, Sheeran stopped being so cautious and even knocked the kangaroo to the ground a few times, but the blows from its tail started to take a toll on him. After the second round, Sheeran asked his buddies in the corner what was hitting him in the back of the head. One of them said it was the referee. Once the third round started, Sheeran hit the kangaroo, only to be slammed in the back of the head with its tail. Thinking the referee had hit him, Sheeran turned and walloped him with an uppercut. He ended up sleeping it off in jail that night.

The next day, he still had Mary in his thoughts. He showed up at her home to ask her out as soon as he was released from the jail cell. She said yes, and they ended up married in short order, much to her parents' displeasure. Sheeran attributed some of this to class issues. According to him, her parents saw his family as "shanty Irish," while he described them as "lace doily Irish." This might have been part of it, but given Sheeran's spotty work record and frequent drunkenness, he likely gave them enough reasons to dislike him; and with some of his later actions, such as drunkenly trying to return the wedding gifts from her side of the family at the reception due to their dislike of him, it might have been warranted.

Regardless of his in-laws' feelings, the newlyweds ended up moving in with her parents. She was working as a secretary at the time, while Sheeran still did odd jobs, working as a bouncer at a dance hall being his main form of employment at the time. He had also borrowed money from four different financing companies in order to pay for the wedding, and when their collectors had come to find him, he convinced them that they didn't find him, using his imposing size to get them to back off.

One of the collector's supervisors wasn't persuaded enough by this and tried to track him down at the dance hall he bounced at. Not knowing what Sheeran looked like, the man-made the mistake of asking Sheeran, who was working the door, if he could show him to Frank Sheeran. Sheeran agreed and took the man towards the men's room. Once inside, Sheeran beat him into unconsciousness.

On the job front, Sheeran's luck soon changed. He noticed a man loading sides of beef into a truck and, realizing that he could easily physically do that, asked the man who to talk to for a job. He soon started working in a meatpacking plant, loading trucks. It was a start and enough to move out of his in-law's home and to get an apartment with Mary, who was pregnant with their first child at the time. Soon, packing the trucks turned into a union truck driving job with the Supermarket Chain Food Fair, a job Sheeran would hold for over 10 years.

Quickly settling into his new job, Sheeran was soon instructed on how easy it was to steal from his employer. He had befriended the man he had noticed packing sides of beef into a truck, and that man showed him that he could take a couple of chickens out of a crate, replacing them with ice to keep the crate the same weight and sell the chickens. He knew a great place to do this, and soon Sheeran was regularly selling several chickens from his runs.

With his steady work, including the money on the side from his pilfered chickens, life was good for Sheeran and his young family. His wife left her job as a secretary and gave birth to their first daughter, then two more over the next couple of years. Frank started supplementing his illegal income by selling football lottery tickets for a racket run by Joey McGreal, the local Teamster boss.

Things took a turn away from domestic bliss when Sheeran started to spend more and more time in downtown Philadelphia. Many of the other drivers for Food Fair were Italian-Americans or Italian immigrants; and given Sheeran's time in Italy during the war, he started to bond with some of them, hanging out in the restaurants and clubs downtown, which reminded him of the cafes in Rome he had enjoyed when not in combat.

As he spent more and more time with his new Italian friends, he went homeless and less. He didn't realize until later just how much he was neglecting his family. He kept giving them money, but he fell further and further into a new life downtown.

He had mentioned his chicken trick to his new friends and soon discovered that he was only dealing in penny-ante theft. Soon, the Italian drivers showed him how to steal whole sides of beef and who to sell them to for the best price. The stockyard manager at the meatpacking plant would place an aluminum cable seal over the lock to prevent the drivers from opening the trucks, and the manager of the store getting the delivery would break the seal. Some stockyard managers were lazy, and often let the drivers seal the truck themselves. Sheeran could deliver some of the meat to the person whose name his new Italian friends gave him and then seal the truck. Sheeran once even sold an entire shipment of beef and delivered an empty, yet sealed truck.

Soon, his new friends started to take him to the Friendly Lounge, owned by a man named Felix "Skinny Razor" DiTullio. According to DiTullio's children, he was given the name "Skinny Razor" for his thin build and his habit of dressing sharply. Sheeran was told that he earned it at his old job as a butcher, where he would use a thin straight razor to decapitate chickens before packing them for purchase. Most historians contend that he earned that title by using a straight razor as his chosen weapon because Felix "Skinny Razor" DiTullio was a feared mafia assassin, second-in-command to the leader of the Philadelphia Mafia, Angelo Bruno, and would later be mentor to the much bloodier Philly Mob Boss Nicodemo "Little Nicky" Scarfo. Sheeran didn't know it then, but he was spending more and more of his time with mafiosos. The Friendly Lounge was a mafia 101 for aspiring criminals, and Sheeran was acing his entrance exam.

In addition to increasing his graft with his job, he started to work as a loan shark for Skinny Razor. Sheeran didn't see this as loan sharking, preferring the term pushing money. He justified these actions because this was before credit cards or payday loans. According to him, these small loans let people go about their lives when times were tough, but at a significant interest rate. Given Little Razor's reputation and what Sheeran would soon discover about his new friends, the rationalization of his actions here is dubious at best.

Sheeran's bosses at Food Fair were starting to suspect him of theft and began to watch him closer. This did little to stop his actions, but they eventually led to his arrest for interstate theft. They had hoped that he would talk and give up the others in the theft ring, especially on the demand side and who was buying the burgled beef. Sheeran didn't talk and made sure to let others in the ring know that he wouldn't talk. He also took the time to break into the offices at the Food Fair and steal a copy of information showing the exact amount of missing product and how it was much greater than just his truck. Claiming that someone placed the information in his mailbox, he was able to use it in the case. The government witnesses clammed up as well, leading to his exoneration.

Food Fair offered him $25,000 to resign, but he refused and continued working and stealing. With the union rules at the time, the only way he could be fired was if they proved that he stole from them. As long as they could not prove it, he could keep his job. Food Fair didn't take this lying down, however, and soon hired a private detective agency to investigate the ring. They caught the man who took the meat from the trucks, packed it into his own, and made the drops. Food Fair offered his freedom for Sheeran's resignation. He tried to get the $25,000 as well, but that part of the deal was off the table by then. To save his co-conspirator, Sheeran quit his job.

Now without his major source of income, he started spending more and more time hanging out with his mafia friends downtown. He could sometimes find short work at the union hall, filling in for sick drivers and the like; but without his Food Fair job, he couldn't push money or a lottery ticket, and he needed more. His imposing size brought some interesting offers from the people who hung out at the Friendly Lounge. He was first offered money to scare a man away from a relative's girlfriend. The man gave him a gun to flash but instructed him not to use it. From there, Sheeran moved into the enforcement side of the loan sharking business. He began to earn a reputation as an en-forcer. Frank Sheeran was beginning to get noticed by those in charge of the whole racket.

# Chapter 3: Hitman for Russell Bufalino

FRANK SHEERAN'S CONNECTIONS with the mafia all center around a single figure: Russell Bufalino. He was known as the Quiet Don for his management style that dealt with issues that arose in his family's business in a way that didn't bring unwanted attention. Born as Rosario Alberto Bufalino on September 25th, 1903, in Montedoro on the island of Sicily in Italy, his family soon emigrated to the United States and settled in Buffalo, New York. Like many Sicilian immigrants, he soon found himself involved in the mafia as he grew up. He had arrests for loan sharking, theft, selling drugs, illegal gambling—all standard rackets for the mafia at the time—though many in the mafia shied away from the selling of drugs, at least back then.

Once prohibition became law, he shifted his criminal business into bootlegging. The families that controlled border areas such as Buffalo and Chicago, found this period especially lucrative and began to focus more and more on the smuggling of alcohol into the United States from Canada. Bufalino soon allied himself with Joseph "Joe the Barber" Barbara, who, at the time, was the underboss of the Northeastern Pennsylvania family, which controlled mafia businesses in Eastern Pennsylvania, except Philadelphia, as well as western upstate New York. Soon, Joe the Barber would have his boss, John Sciandra, killed and take over the family. The North-Eastern Pennsylvania family held almost complete control of the local coal mining and Teamster's unions, along with the other standard mafia rackets in the area. Bufalino moved up with Joe the Barber, becoming his underboss.

The Mafia in America was largely modeled off of the original Mafia that controlled many of the criminal enterprises in Italy through their base on the island of Sicily. This isn't to say that all organized crime was run by Sicilian immigrants. On the contrary, ethnically connected gangs of criminals began to become more organized in the 19th century. Irish and Jewish gangs were common in New York, with the Jewish gangs becoming powerful allies to the Italian Mafia in the early 20th century and beyond. Tongs and Triads were common in any major American city with a large China Town, and African American gangs often held sway in their segregated communities. The Sicilian Mafia had an advantage in their rules and organization, which enabled them to become the dominant organized criminal gang.

Under the rules used in Sicily was the concept that all the Sicilian mafia groups deferred to a single boss, the Capo di Tutti Capi, or Boss of Bosses. This leader usually took power over having it granted and was responsible for setting the rules that the other mafia families would follow and for enforcing the often lethal consequences for breaking these rules. Prior to 1931, this was how the American Mafia was run. Prohibition led to great changes to that model.

For the Mafia, prohibition was a gift. Despite being made illegal, alcohol was still popular with a large portion of the population, and the Mafia was in a perfect place to supply illegal alcohol to this giant market. The Mafia in cities like Chicago and Buffalo, near the border with Canada, became more important. However, the increase in Mafia operations led to its ranks swelling dramatically. Many of the newer members of the Mafia families found the old world rules and traditions taken directly from the Sicilian mafia stifling. The old world Sicilian mafia refused to work with non-Italians, which became a giant limitation in a multicultural city like New York.

The lucrative nature of the American Mafia's business under prohibition came under the notice of the leaders of the Mafia in Sicily as well. Some of these Dons wanted a piece of the pie for themselves. Don Vito Ferro sent Salvatore Maranzano to the United States in a bid to take over as the Boss of Bosses of the American Mafia. This led to what was called the Castellammarese War, as Marazano and those who followed him went to war with, Joe "The Boss" Masseria for the title of Boss of Bosses. This was a deadly war that involved almost every major mafia figure at the time. At its end, Marazano won when Lucky Luciano, a young up and coming Mafioso, who had been serving on Masseria's side, had his boss killed.

Instead of running as it had before the Castellammarese War, now with Marazano as the new Boss of Bosses, Luciano had Marazano killed as well. Ironically, the hit on the more traditional Sicilian Don was handled by Jewish gangsters hired by Meyer Lansky and Benjamin "Bugsy" Siegel, two close allies of Luciano.

Luciano turned away from the Boss of Bosses model and formed the Mafia Commission. With this, the American Mafia was organized more like a corporation. It formalized the control of New York City under the five mafia families, a structure that still exists today, though some of the families have changed hands. The heads of these families took a seat on the council with the head of the Chicago Outfit and the Buffalo Family also receiving a place on the board. All other cities were limited to a single Mafia family and represented on the board through the existing board members.

The commission had veto power over new bosses and made some changes to the rules the American Mafia ran under. This included allowing the Jewish mobsters, like Siegel and Lansky, to work more closely with the Mafia. Almost from the start, the commission found itself split into two factions: a conservative faction of older Dons who wanted to keep more of the traditions from the old world and a liberal faction that sought to remove these restrictions, especially when in doing so, they could make more money and seize more power. The illegal sale of drugs was an example of the disagreements between the two factions.

The objection to the drug trade by the conservative faction was not a moral or ethical objection but an attempt to keep their illicit business secret. Prohibition allowed the Mafia to grow exponentially, but it also brought with it a lot of visibility. When prohibition ended, taking with it a great deal of the Mafia's revenue, they needed to replace that business—and with over a decade of experience smuggling alcohol, they had an existing infrastructure that could be used with other, still prohibited, drugs. The conservative faction held control until after the second world war when the liberals started making gains.

By the 50s, Vito Genovese had taken control of the Luciano Family and attempted to take control of the New York families and become a new Boss of Bosses. This led to more in fighting on the commission, which, at that point, was expanding to include the Philadelphia Family, Los Angeles Family, and Detroit Partnership. Genovese called for a meeting of the American Mafia, ostensibly, to discuss several issues that the mafia was dealing with at the time, but he also wanted the meeting as a way to legitimize his position as Boss of Bosses. Joe the Barber offered his country home in Apalachin, New York, for the summit.

One hundred and one leaders of the American Mafia, representing every major Mafia family as well as mafiosos from both Canada and Italy, made their way to the meeting. Bufalino, as Joe the Barber's underboss, took part in organizing it. Unfortunately for the mobsters invited, Joe, the Barber's son, was overheard reserving some local hotel rooms by a New York State trooper named Edgar D. Croswell. He investigated and discovered dozens of luxury cars parked at Joe the Barber's home. Once he checked a couple of the license plates, he discovered some of them belonged to known criminals. The police surrounded the property, setting up roadblocks and raiding the meeting. Dozens of Mafia leaders fled through the woods and escaped, but over 50 were captured, including Joe the Barber, Russell Bufalino, and several members of the leadership of the different families.

This raid brought a level of unwanted attention to the mafia that they had never had to deal with and put them on the map with the federal government in a way they have never fully recovered from. For Bufalino, however, it led to him gaining more control. Joe the Barber unofficially retired, allowing Bufalino to take over the North East Pennsylvania Family, now known as the Bufalino Crime Family. Under his quiet leadership, the family prospered, expanding during the 60s and 70s, taking over the Buffalo Family and using its influence to gain lucrative and legitimate arms contracts during the Vietnam War. Bufalino often held greater national sway than his small regional operation would normally be allocated. Bufalino was described by Genovese Crime Family member Joseph Valachi, the first American Mafia member to admit to its existence, in congressional testimony as, "one of the most ruthless and powerful leaders of the Mafia in the United States."

Sheeran first met Bufalino when he was still driving trucks for Food Fair, a few years before the Apalachin meeting. On a delivery trip to Syracuse, New York, Sheeran's truck broke down in at a truck stop along the way. An older Italian gentleman approached him as he worked on the truck and offered his help. He began fiddling under the hood, and the two started to chat, with Bufalino impressed by Sheeran's knowledge of Italian. Sheeran had no idea who he was getting help from, thinking at the time that he might have been the owner of the truck stop.

Their next meeting occurred at Sheeran's normal downtown hang out: The Friendly Lounge. Sheeran noticed Bufalino talking with Angelo Bruno, the boss of the Philadelphia Family, though Sheeran did not know this at the time. Once his meeting with Bruno concluded, Bufalino greeted Sheeran and mentioned that he always came to Philadelphia for the Prosciutto Bread, a local favorite consisting of bread baked with prosciutto ham and cheese inside. Sheeran made a point to deliver some Prosciutto Bread to Bufalino when his Food Fair route took him near Bufalino's home. They soon became friends and bonded over Sheeran's wartime visit to Sicily, where he had briefly stayed in Bufalino's hometown of Montedoro.

When Sheeran quit his Food Fair job to keep his co-conspirator in the theft ring out of trouble, the respect he was shown at the Friendly Lounge skyrocketed. He wasn't Italian, so he couldn't be a full member of the mafia, but his actions showed that he was trustworthy. His friendship with the powerful Bufalino, though he still did not know he was a mafia leader, added to the respect he was shown. As he started working more and more for the Mafia figures that frequented the Friendly Lounge, he earned the nickname Cheech, short for the Italian version of his first name: Francesco.

Bufalino would often call Sheeran and have him act as his driver as he moved around his territory, handling business that couldn't be handled over the phone. Sheeran received no payment from these chauffeur jobs, but he understood that there was a benefit from being seen with Bufalino, and he was about to learn why. Sheeran drove Bufalino to Joe the Barber's house in Appalachian before the infamous mafia summit. The next day, he saw his friend's name in the paper as one of the mafiosos that were arrested. Sheeran now knew the type of people he had been spending so much time with, but it didn't make him rethink his actions.

Sheeran continued to frequent the Friendly Lounge, where he had been taking more enforcement jobs— "errands," he called them—where he would threaten someone whose loan payments were late. Most of the time, he only had to flash a gun to get the point across. Bufalino stopped showing up for a while after the bust. Sheeran assumed he was laying low until the heat was off of him.

One of Skinny Razor's loan sharks by the name of Whispers approached Sheeran with a ten-thousand-dollar offer. They agreed to meet in an out-of-the-way cafe to discuss the details. Whispers handled bigger loans that were given to businesses, as opposed to the smaller loans that Sheeran had handled when he had his Food Fair route. One of the Whispers' clients, a linen company, was having problems paying back the loan. Most of the time, they were only paying the interest; sometimes they failed to pay even that, but Whispers had a plan.

He wanted Sheeran to put their main competition, Cadillac Linen Services, out of business permanently. He gave Sheeran two thousand dollars upfront and would give him the other eight after it was finished, instructing him to not talk about it to anyone. Not one to waste time, Sheeran cased the building, planning on burning it down and devising the best way to have it burnt to the ground before the fire department could respond. The day after he cased the Cadillac Linen Services building, he went to the Friendly Lounge as he usually did, but something was off. Skinny Razor came right over to him and said he was needed in the back. Sheeran realized that the doorman behind him had moved to block his exit. Not knowing what the problem was and having little choice, Sheeran followed Skinny razor to the back.

In the backroom, he found Angelo Bruno sitting next to his old friend, Russell Bufalino. Bruno demanded to know what Sheeran was doing outside of the Cadillac Linen Services building. Realizing the potential danger he was in, Sheeran told Bruno everything, including Whispers' offer and his potential plan to burn it down. Shaking his head, Bruno informed Sheeran that Cadillac Linen Services was owned by the Jewish mob. Sheeran realized that Whispers' offer put him in the targets of the Jewish gangsters. Whispers might be better able to collect on his overdue loan, but when the Jews came for retribution, they would have come straight at Sheeran.

Bufalino excused himself, after which Bruno told Sheeran he owed his life to his friend Bufalino. Had Bufalino not vouched for Sheeran, Bruno would have let the Jews kill him. Before letting him go, Bruno instructed him to take care of the problem. Sheeran understood the message and made arrangements with Whispers to meet and discuss the job. He shot and killed Whispers with the .32 caliber gun he was initially given in his first collection job. The next day, when he went to the Friendly Lounge, Bruno gave him his meal on the house, and everyone looked at him differently. He had killed for the first time since the liberation of Dachau, and as far as the mafiosos of eastern Pennsylvania were concerned, he was one of them now.

Many things changed as a result of his murder of Whispers. He started taking a bigger role in the loan sharking run by Skinny Razor, and he began to carry a gun wherever he went. His already frayed relationship with his wife further deteriorated as well. He moved out of the house and closer to downtown. He still sent child support to his wife, but he had distanced himself almost completely.

Another aspect of the mafia business that he became more involved in was murder. The Mafia didn't kill indiscriminately, and even when they did kill, it was a last resort. The murder was loud, and dead bodies—even those of gangsters and thugs—bring unwanted police attention. Still, they sometimes needed to send a message to deter others from moving against them. Sheeran began to handle these problems, killing low-level Mafia members for stealing from Bruno or Bufalino. By this point, Bufalino had given Sheeran the name: The Irishman, a name that overtook Cheech as his nickname among the gangsters.

Even with the increased work from his mafia friends, Sheeran's income was too erratic. He would go through periods of feasts and famines. As he still gave a lot of his money as child support, he was in need of a more regular paycheck. Bufalino had an idea for him. Sheeran had always been a union man, so he should look to moving up in the union. Given the makeup of the local union, Sheeran didn't see an opening for him. Bufalino had a solution and called up the national leader of the Teamsters union: Jimmy Hoffa.

# Chapter 4: Muscle for Jimmy Hoffa's Teamsters

LABOR UNIONS AND THE mafia have a colorful history that, in some ways, dates back to the very start of the labor union movements. The labor unions were one of the many consequences of the radical changes to society caused by the industrial revolution. Advancements in technology during the latter half of the 18th century and continuing through the 19th century moved the manufacturing of goods from the hands of artisans to an increasingly mechanized process. This led to a much greater output with lower production costs. Agricultural methods also underwent radical changes, allowing for greater yields and enabling farms to produce much more food while using a fraction of the labor.

Prior to industrialization, the majority of people worked in agriculture in some way, and when machines were able to make that work more efficient, those people found work in the factories that sprung up, taking part in the making of these new manufacturing products; or in the mines, digging the coal that was fueling the industrial revolution. The changes brought by the industrial revolution led to a population boom, providing these new factories cheaper and cheaper labor.

At the time, there were few protections for workers. Factories could be dangerous and even deadly places, while the coal mines were even deadlier. By the latter half of the 19th century, employers took great advantage of their workforces. Long hours for low pay were common in many industries. More dangerous occupations, such as mining, came with little in the way of safety rules or protections. Some companies would even pay their workers in scrip instead of cash. This script could only be used in the company store, where the selection was small and the prices artificially high.

These conditions led to great discontent among the workers in several of the industries that treated their employees the worst. The law at this time heavily favored the industrialists over the workers. A landmark 1905 Supreme Court case, Lochner v. New York, established a legal view that the states could not make laws that would infringe on the right to contract. This included laws that established a minimum wage or laws that would make it illegal to require someone to work more than 10 hour days.

Workers began to organize and started staging strikes. Companies would react to these early labor strikes severely and often with great violence. The Pinkerton National Detective Agency, an early private security company, was often hired to help break up these strikes as well as to infiltrate the workers and their fledgling unions. The unions themselves often used violence in response. Strikebreakers or scabs, workers who continued to work during a strike, were often attacked by picketers on their way into the factory or mines. The Pinkertons would be on hand to protect the strikebreakers, and some unions would hire criminals and gangsters to protect their picketers.

In the first half of the 20th century, laws started to change, and unions grew in power—helping to establish labor norms, such as the 8-hour workday and the minimum wage. One of the more powerful unions that started at the turn of the twentieth century was the Teamsters. The term "Teamster" comes from the name of the workers who drove teams of animals involved in the moving of goods from factories or from the docks. As the internal combustion engine led to trucks replacing horses, the Teamster Union rose to represent truck drivers.

By the start of the 20th century, steamships and railroads had made the movement of goods worldwide a much faster and cheaper process than ever before. Truck drivers performed an important role in this process, and the Teamster's prominence rose accordingly. Unions often fought between themselves during this era as they worked to gain more power and prominence. The Teamsters were often at odds with the Longshoreman Unions that controlled the labor on the docks—loading and unloading ships. Both unions worked in the transportation of goods, so it was natural that there would be some overlap.

Organized crime was another problem for unions, in general, and the Teamsters in particular. Unions involved with the transportation of goods were particularly good targets for the mafia, as they can be used for the smuggling of goods, but that was only a fraction of the benefits the mafia could obtain from controlling unions. Prior to the late 1950s, union finances were generally secret, allowing mafia-controlled local unions to steal from the union dues. Extortion was one of the more common mafia rackets. Requiring a local business to pay protection money is an example of this common in mafia literature and film. With control of a union, the mafia could extort businesses that rely on the union for services by threatening strikes or work slow-downs that would negatively affect them. The five mafia families in New Your City, for example, long-held control of the city's concrete businesses. If a builder did not pay them off, they would have problems getting concrete to their site.

One of the more galling usages of mafia-controlled unions was through paper locals. A paper local was a local branch of a union that existed only on paper. Unions have used these in the past when organizing a new union. They would create the union on paper, and once the workers voted to join, they would just sign the people up. Less reputable unions have used them in order to add fake votes to union elections, turning the tide for their chosen candidates. The Mafia sometimes used paper unions when setting up sweetheart deals with nonunion shops. In these situations, the paper union negotiates a new contract with the company, but instead of the benefits from this new contract going to the workers, the mafia and business owner split it between themselves. For example, the paper local and Company X negotiates for a $2 raise for the workers. The workers get paid the same, and the paper local and company X each take a dollar for every worker.

For the unions, having mafia involved was not a complete negative for them. The intimidation factor alone could bring more companies under union control. Fighting between unions was a common problem in the early days, and having mafia support for your union could make the difference. The Mafia was also more willing than regular union members to commit crimes in furtherance of the union's power. Getting in bed with the mafia was a devil's bargain, but it was not without benefit.

Due to the potential advantages of controlling local unions, the mafia worked to bring many of them under their control. This happened in many ways. Having men under the control of a mafia family join the union and work their way up was one way, but as was often the case with the mafia, threats and bribes often work the best, especially when the leadership of the union itself was corrupt. For the Teamsters, corruption became a major issue when their longtime president stepped down and was replaced by Dave Beck, while Jimmy Hoffa began working to take control of the union.

Jimmy Hoffa's family moved to Detroit when he was very young. His father died before he was 10, and he left school at the age of 14 in order to start working to support his widowed mother and family. His union-organizing stint began soon after. While working in a grocery store as a teen, he began to organize his fellow workers into a union. His actions in organizing that union brought him the attention of the local Teamsters union, who offered him a job with the union as an organizer. He met his eventual wife through this work while organizing strikes at a local laundry.

Hoffa rapidly moved up the ranks and was instrumental in the expansion of the union. His ability to organize secondary boycotts, where other unions support strikers by refusing to use products or services of the company the strike is against, as well as quick strikes brought more and more shipping companies under the Teamsters union. This work often brought him into close contact with mafia-controlled locals, which he used to his advantage, muscling out other unions and disposing of problematic members. In return, he granted them no-show union jobs and offered other financial incentives for support.

When Dave Beck took over as president of the Teamsters Union, Hoffa worked his mafia connections in order to try and wrest control of the union from him. One of the ways he had planned to do this was through the use of several paper locals voting his way. His plans to do this in New York City, with the help of mafioso Johnny Dio became public, led to US Senate Hearings headed by Senator John L. McClellan, though Senator Bobby Kennedy was given control over the hearings. Dave Beck fled the country to avoid a subpoena and did not appear in court; he "took the Fifth" one hundred and seventeen times.

Hoffa attempted to use the Committee against Beck. He recruited Beck's lawyer and used him to provide information on Beck's illegal activity to the investigators. He also attempted to put an informant into the investigation. He had approached a young lawyer and asked him to apply to the committee as an investigator, offering him money for information he would gain. The lawyer informed the FBI instead, and they went through a sting operation in order to arrest Hoffa.

A week after that, it came out that Beck had taken a $300,000 interest-free loan from the Teamsters, and he was soon removed from his position. Hoffa, though plagued by scandal, ended up beating the bribery charges, ostensibly by using the race card. Washington, DC, had a large African American population. Hoffa's lawyers worked to have a majority African American jury and made Hoffa out to be a "Champion of the Negros." He used his connection to the Chicago Outfit to bring the retired boxer Joe Lewis to the courtroom to offer Hoffa his support. Afterward, Lewis, who was down on his luck, obtained a well-paying job with a record company that just happened to have been given a loan by the Teamsters. Hoffa also took out advertisements in African American magazines and papers in order to build his support among their community. The ploy worked, and he was acquitted—though he was under a legal cloud.

As a result of the McClellan Hearings, new laws were put into place that required unions to disclose what they do with their member's dues. Hoffa had a card up his sleeve for this situation, however, in the teamster's pension plan. This plan took in payments from the members as well as the companies that employed union members, and under Hoffa, this fund became a de facto private bank for the mafia. The Teamsters would loan out money to fund various mafia projects, such as the casinos in Havana and Las Vegas.

Frank Sheeran first came into contact with Jimmy Hoffa soon after he took control of the Teamsters in the aftermath of the McClellan Hearings. Russell Bufalino called Hoffa and passed the phone to Sheeran. Hoffa's first words to Sheeran were, "I heard you paint houses." This was mafia code at the time for killing people to which the stammering Sheeran answered that he did his own carpentry. Hoffa offered Sheeran a position with the Teamsters union on the spot and instructed him to be in Detroit the next day. Sheeran planned to drive, but Bufalino gave him a bag containing a plane ticket and a stack of hundred-dollar bills before taking him out for a going-away dinner.

Sheeran flew to Detroit with dreams of being an international union organizer in his head. He imagined a life where he could help others build local unions all over the country and get away from the life of crime he had been living. He was assigned to an organizing team that was dealing with unionizing the local cabbies, and for a few weeks, he helped spread information about the union among the cabbies and took part in the organization of the picket lines, then came the Chicago Job.

One of Hoffa's mob allies and labor organizers in Chicago, Joey Glimco, had a problem that needed a "house painter" to solve. The leader of Sheeran's organizing group asked him out of the blue about "painting houses." Nobody in the business ever directly talked about killing. And after Sheeran admitted he was familiar, he soon found himself on a plane for a three-hour trip to Chicago. The hit needed to be public, so a lot of planning went into pulling it off and getting away. Sheeran was met at the airport by a driver who took him where he needed to be and gave him the gun. Once the deed was done, Sheeran handed the gun off to another man who would leave the scene and deconstruct the gun, destroying it or disposing of it in multiple places. Sheeran got into another car that was driven away from the scene and then back to the airport, while other cars were already placed in the area to block any pursuit from the cops.

Sheeran recalled the relief he felt when they made it back to the airport. One of the best ways to get away with a hit is to kill the hitter. Sheeran had been around the mafia for long enough to know that they are more than willing to remove a potential issue before it became one. Leaving the scene of his first murder for the Teamsters, Sheeran worried that they might be taking him to an abandoned warehouse on the docks to "paint his house," too.

For his position in Hoffa's inner circle, the Chicago job was an audition of sorts. And with it successfully concluded, he found himself with much more work, both in labor organizing and in taking care of problems for Hoffa. He began to split his time between the Detroit home office, along with Chicago and

Philadelphia, though he often took short trips to deal with Hoffa's problems.

Hoffa often visited when he was in Chicago, and Sheeran soon became aquatinted with the major mafia figures in the Chicago Outfit. Hoffa's main contact there, Joey Glimco, was a Soldier for Al Capone in the 20s and 30s when he ran the Outfit, but Sheeran also met Sam "Momo" Giancana, the leader of the Chicago Outfit. Giancana could not be more different from Bufalino. Giancana flashed his wealth and power, often spending time with celebrities, while Bufalino stayed quiet and behind the scenes. Giancana was occasionally visited by his man in Dallas, a man by the name of Jack Ruby.

As the election of 1960 came closer, a split formed as to which candidate to support between Hoffa and his Mafia allies. Bobby Kennedy was in charge of the McClellan hearings and had tried his hardest to convict Hoffa. This left Hoffa with a great hatred for the man, so instead of supporting his brother John Kennedy, the Teamsters became the only major union to support Richard Nixon.

The mafia had their own problems with Bobby Kennedy, the McClellan hearings looked into the mafia as well, but Giancana had connections with Joseph Kennedy, JFK, and RFK's father, that went back years. Joseph Kennedy made a great deal of money bootlegging during prohibition, working alongside many members of the mafia that had risen to the tops of the ranks by the late 50s. Giancana had spoken to Joseph Kennedy and received assurances that Bobby would be held in check when it came to the mafia.

On the other hand, Nixon was the vice president for Eisenhower, whom the mafia blamed for the loss of their Cuban assets when Castro came into power. In the 50s, the Mafia started to build resorts and casinos in Havana. Castro's communist revolution led to the seizure of these resorts and casinos, costing the mafia a great deal of money and other resources. Giancana hoped that Kennedy would do more to get rid of Castro and return Cuba to its pre-revolutionary government.

The 1960 election was one of the closest presidential elections in American History, with the final vote totaling 34,220,984 for Kennedy and 34,108,157 for Nixon, a difference of less than a quarter of a point. Giancana did what he needed to do to make sure that Illinois went for Kennedy, allegations of voter fraud in Chicago started almost immediately after the election, though Nixon chose not to fight the results. Kennedy won and installed his brother Bobbie as Attorney General. The new Attorney General made it his goal to take Jimmy Hoffa down.

# Chapter 5: Supplying Arms for the Bay of Pigs Invasion and the Assassination of JFK

THE MAFIA APPROACHED the incoming Kennedy administration with both apprehension and hope. They knew Kennedy's father from his time as a bootlegger during prohibition. Sam Giancana had made contacts with the Kennedy campaign, using Frank Sinatra as a go-between, helping Kennedy in both the West Virginia primary and in the general election in Illinois. Sinatra was a good choice for this because he had strong mafia ties, his family came from the same town in Sicily that Lucky Luciano was born in, and they became friends when Sinatra was younger. As an entertainer, Sinatra could also easily be seen in the company of the Kennedys. Sinatra and Jack Kennedy had a mistress in common, as well. Bufalino never liked Sinatra, and from the times he met him, Sheeran himself was no fan. He considered Sinatra an angry drunkard.

Joe Kennedy had promised that Jack could keep Bobby in check during his administration and that the Administration would help with the mafia's problems related to Cuba after Castro took over. On the other hand, JFK had given his brother the position of Attorney General, making him the number one law enforcement agency in the country. Bobby, as a senator taking control of the McClellan Hearings on corruption in organized labor, had made Jimmy Hoffa his number one target, failing three times to convict him of a variety of crimes. This commission had also probed the many connections between the Teamsters and the mafia.

Many in the Mafia saw Bobby's elevation to the Attorney General as a broken promise on the part of his father. Bobby went hard against both Hoffa and the Mafia during his time as Attorney General. He created a squad in charge of investigating Hoffa, known as the Get Hoffa Squad. He also instructed all of the agencies involved in federal law enforcement to start sharing information to use it against the mafia efficiently. Mafia convictions rose sharply during the Kennedy Administration.

Still, the prospect of returning Cuba to the pre-Castro regime kept the mafia, and a reluctant Hoffa, working with the Kennedy administration, at least at its onus. Cuba was that important to the Mafia, thanks mostly to Lucky Luciano. Luciano had shifted the American Mafia from the Sicilian, Boss of Bosses' leadership style, to being led by the committee and was one of the major powers in the American Mafia running the Luciano family, one of the five mafia families given control over New York City. Luciano was often at odds with the New York District Attorney, Thomas Dewey. When Dewey was appointed as the US Attorney for the Southern District of New York, he prosecuted Luciano for forcible prostitution relating to the brothels that he ran.

Luciano was convicted and sentenced to 30 to 50 years of jail time. His position as one of the leaders of the American Mafia fell immediately and would have disappeared completely until his luck changed at the onset of the second world war. The CIA approached Meyer Lansky, an ally of Luciano from the Jewish mob, as well as Joseph Lanza, a member of Luciano's mafia family, with an offer. They feared that Nazi saboteurs would be interested in damaging the shipping docks in New York City. Both prior to and during the war, these docks were used extensively to load supplies destined for America's allies in Europe.

To prevent this, the predecessor of the CIA offered Luciano a pardon after the war, with the condition that he was to never return to the United States if he would use the Mafia's control of the ports to watch for Nazi saboteurs. Dewey reluctantly agreed to this, and after the war, Luciano was pardoned and placed on a streamliner destined for Italy. In order to retain control of his mafia organization, Luciano needed a place much closer to the United States than Italy, and he set his eyes on Cuba.

Meyer Lansky was instrumental in this choice. Lansky's criminal career dated back to his teen years when he and his childhood friend, Bugsy Siegel, formed a small Jewish gang in New York during prohibition. Lansky soon met Luciano when the elder Luciano attempted to extort protection money from Lansky and found himself impressed by Lansky's defiant demeanor. Lansky worked with Luciano from that point on, helping Luciano take control of the American Mafia—and using his Jewish gang, that by this point had evolved into the much-feared Murder Incorporated, as Luciano's hit squad for hire.

Lansky's own rackets tended to focus on gambling. He ran a gambling operation in several states and had started looking to Cuba. During the early 40s, Fulgencio Batista became president of Cuba, and Lansky began cultivating a friendship with the man, offering him bribes and kickbacks for allowing the Mafia to gain control of several lucrative businesses in Cuba, including casinos and racetracks. Lansky started investing heavily in Cuba, using dirty money from his illicit activities to fund his new investments. He also brought Luciano into these Cuban moves.

For Luciano, Cuba seemed like a perfect place for him to run his American Mafia empire and moved to the island. Once there, he called a meeting of the American Mafia in Cuba, in part to show his face and power to help him reassert his control over the Mafia. It was a big conference with the leaders of the New York Family, Chicago outfit, Lansky's Jewish mob, and others. Entertainment was provided by Frank Sinatra. Another of the major topics was the mafia expansion on the West Coast, including Las Vegas, where they were building the Flamenco Hotel at the time.

After the conference, the Mafia began to build up casinos and resorts in Cuba, using it as Lansky had, as a way to use their dirty cash without US control. Unfortunately for Luciano, Batista lost the presidency, and the new Cuban government bowed to US pressure and forced Luciano to leave the country. This did little to stop mob involvement in the island, and Batista's fortune changed in the early 50s when he ran for President of Cuba again. Realizing that he was going to lose, he instigated a military coup and took control of the government.

Cuba, under Batista's dictatorship, was as close to a mafia utopia that has ever existed. As the Mafia had paid him off extensively, Batista allowed almost everything. The mafia controlled the casinos and resorts, while drugs and alcohol were readily available for the international tourists that flocked the island, as it became known for its potential for hedonistic pleasure. Batista was aided by the United States government in his coup, and over the course of his regime, several of the major industries of Cuba were slowly ceded to US interests, depriving the Cuban people of their resources.

Batista's actions giving the Mafia carte blanche over the island's vice trade and allowing US interests to take control of the other industries, such as the sugar industry, became one of the rallying cries for Fidel Castro's revolution. The young revolutionary finally succeeded in taking over Batista's government in 1959 and seized control of Mafia resources on the island at that time.

Returning Cuba to its pre-Castro government was one of the promises Joe Kennedy made to Sam Giancana, the leader of the Chicago Outfit, when he secured Mafia assistance in getting Kennedy elected. Hoffa, with his hatred for Bobby Kennedy, reluctantly went along with the Mafia's plans to take Cuba back, though he was still hesitant. For Frank Sheeran, he was of two minds when it came to Kennedy. As an Irish Catholic, Kennedy was popular among Irish Catholic-Americans such as Sheeran. On the other hand, his close friendship and working relationship with Hoffa led Sheeran not to discuss Kennedy in front of him.

In working with Bufalino, Sheeran often accompanied him as his driver. This included driving him to Hollywood, Florida, where Bufalino would meet with the Florida-based Mafia as well as Meyer Lansky to discuss the Cuban issue. Sheeran had little to do with these meetings, other than chauffeuring Bufalino, but he met several figures in Lansky's circle.

The CIA started working with the Mafia soon after Castro came to power, planning the assassination of Castro. The CIA offered the Mafia a return to the pre-Castro days, where they could control the island's vice trades, in return for performing the assassination. Giancana had made plans to poison the new dictator.

Sheeran's involvement with the Mafia's attempt to remove Castro concerned a different aspect of their anti-Castro work. It all started with a call from Jimmy Hoffa when Sheeran was in Philadelphia after Sheeran moved to a payphone out of fear that the phone at the Friendly Lounge might be tapped. Hoffa instructed Sheeran to get himself a clean truck and drive it to a location in Baltimore after calling Bufalino and informing him. Sheeran was able to get a truck from a company that was behind on its loan payment with the Mafia and provided favors in lieu of payments.

Once he arrived at the address in Baltimore, he discovered that it was a warehouse with a small landing strip. A plane sat on the runway, while another truck was parked nearby. As he slowed to a stop, a man came out of the plane. Sheeran recognized him as a pilot he had met when taking Bufalino to meet Lansky in Florida. He motioned Sheeran to pull up next to the other truck. Soldiers appeared from behind the truck and began to unload their contents and to load them in Sheeran's truck. They were Maryland National Guard members, and the cargo they were loading was made up of military weapons, ammunition, and uniforms.

With the truck loaded, they gave Sheeran a manifest with the appropriate paperwork and instructed him to take the truck to a dog track outside of Jacksonville, Florida. Meeting him at the Dog Track was a man named E. Howard Hunt. It was not a name that Sheeran would have recognized, though most of America, Sheeran included, would recognize it less than fifteen years later when E. Howard Hunt became known as one of President Nixon's infamous plumber during the Watergate Hearings. Then, he secretly worked for president Nixon in an attempt to find leaks in the campaign as well as in various illegal acts in support of the president. In the 60s, however, he was a CIA agent, and the truck full of military weapons was en route to a group of anti-Castro Cubans that were about to invade the island.

The planned assassination of Castro, using the mafia, was only one of the plans the United States had to remove the communist dictator. The invasion of Cuba, called the Bay of Pigs Invasion based on the location of the amphibious landing, was the other. Like the planned assassination, Hoffa and the Mafia played a role. Giancana was the main connection between the CIA and the Mafia. As Bufalino was a major ally of Giancana, and Sheeran was one of Bufalino's most trusted men with truck driving experience, it made sense that Sheeran would be involved in the movement of these weapons.

The invasion had been planned by the Eisenhower administration, but Castro took power so late in his administration, that he delayed the plans until the next president was in office. Kennedy was reluctant to put the plan into action but eventually agreed to do so. The invasion started promisingly. the 1,400 anti-Castro Cubans gathered in Guatemala and then struck at the beaches of the Bay of Pigs on the Southside of the island. The plan required air support for success, and the US provided it on the first day of the invasion, allowing the anti-Castro Cubans to gain an advantage.

Unfortunately for the anti-Castro Cubans, as the invasion became known to the other powers of the world, Kennedy became reluctant to continue with the air support. Castro rallied his revolutionary forces and brought a swift end to the invasion. The involvement of the United States in the Bay of Pigs Invasion caused Castro's communist government to ally itself more closely with the Soviet Union and gave Castro a much stronger hold over Cuba.

While the CIA under Kennedy was trying to take out Castro, Bobby Kennedy was using the power of his position as Attorney General to put Jimmy Hoffa in prison as well as go after other mafia figures. The inclusion of the IRS in his pooling of information enabled him to target several prominent mafia figures based on their failure to pay income taxes. This was the same way the federal government was able to put Al Capone of the Chicago Outfit into jail. It is one of the ironies of the income tax—in order to be in compliance, you must list your illicit income.

Hoffa had been in Bobby Kennedy's sights since his time on the McClellan committee. He had tried Hoffa three times for various crimes, and Hoffa beat the charges each time. As Attorney General, he tried a fourth time with charges based on the creation of a dummy corporation in his wife's name. He, along with another Teamster leader, had created the company, and it had major contracts with other Teamster companies for over one million dollars. There were no allegations that the company didn't provide services for these contracts. It leased its small fleet of trucks for it, but the way it was formed could have broken a misdemeanor statute.

Instead of fighting the charges in court, Hoffa wanted more certainty, and multiple jurors were forced off the jury when bribes were reported. The first juror to come forward claimed that his neighbor offered him ten thousand dollars for an acquittal. Several jurors came forward afterward, claiming that a reporter from a local paper had called asking them their views on the case. When investigated, no reporter of the name given worked for the paper. An African American juror was offered ten thousand dollars by a Detroit-based African-American business-man with close ties to Hoffa. A third juror was removed from the case when the prosecution discovered that some Teamsters offered her husband, a Tennessee State Trooper, ten thousand dollars for an acquittal. They had the man followed and watched them hand over the money.

Hoffa brought Sheeran to the courtroom after these jurors were removed. Form Sheeran's perspective, he was there to intimidate the other jurors who had been bribed from coming forward and exposing those bribes. No other juror came forward after that, and the trial ended with a hung jury.

Bobby Kennedy had an ace up his sleeve, though, in Grady Partin. Partin was a Teamster and had a role in Hoffa's inner circle, but he also reported Hoffa's action to Bobby Kennedy's justice department. This included discussions where Hoffa planned to assassinate Bobby Kennedy with a bomb when he continued his crusade against Hoffa. When President Kennedy learned about this, he wanted it released to the public to persuade Hoffa to give up his assassination plans. Bobby thought differently and wanted to continue to use Partin to gain more information on Hoffa's plans. In the end, Kennedy used this information to charge Hoffa with jury tampering.

The failed Bay of Pigs Invasion spurred Castro towards the Soviets, but it also pushed the mafia away from Kennedy. Hoffa's issues with Bobby Kennedy meant that he was against his brother's administration from before the beginning. The Kennedy administration was led by an acrimonious group. Kennedy fought a contentious primary campaign against the southern Democrat, Lyndon Baines Johnson—but as he won that primary, he realized that as a Northern Catholic, he needed Johnson on the ticket to win the south. Hence, he offered him the vice presidency. Bobby was Kennedy's most trusted confidant, and that position caused problems between him and Johnson. Hoffa and the Mafia came to the conclusion that without Jack Kennedy in the White House, a president Johnson would quickly replace Bobby Kennedy.

The JFK assassination has been one of the most studied, and some might say overstudied, events of the 20th century. The official story is that Lee Harvey Oswald, a man who spent a great deal of time in the Soviet Union, shot President Kennedy in Dallas as his motorcade passed the Texas School Book Depository, where Oswald took the shots from. He was arrested that day after killing a police officer in his attempt to flee. The next day, Jack Ruby, a man with known mafia ties, whom Sheeran had met while meeting Sam Giancana in Chicago. Sheeran took a phone call from Hoffa in the early days of November 1963, where Hoffa instructed him to visit Bufalino. Bufalino, for his part, told Sheeran to pay the Genovese family in New York City a visit. The Genovese family used to be the Luciano Family before Vito Genovese seized control of it while Luciano was in his exile in Italy.

Sheeran made the trip as requested and was given a duffel bag with three rifles in it. From there, he made his way to the same airstrip in Baltimore, meeting the same pilot as before. Sheeran returned to Bufalino and went about his business, as usual, finding himself as shocked as most of every other American when the news of Kennedy's death came out but a bit less surprising when Jack Ruby killed Oswald.

Hoffa might have been overjoyed that Kennedy was dead, thinking Bobby would be out of a job. Johnson and Bobby were able to look past their differences, however, and the prosecution of Hoffa for jury tampering continued and eventually led to his imprisonment.

# Chapter 6: The Murder of Crazy Joe Gallo

ON APRIL 7, 1972, AT 4:30 in the morning, a small group of people entered Umberto's Clam House in the Little Italy neighborhood of Manhattan. It included Joe Gallo—known as Crazy Joe—as well as his wife, his daughter, his sister, and his bodyguard. They were celebrating his 43rd birthday. Gallo had been released from prison the year before and had found a level of celebrity that most mafiosos shy away from.

Soon after he was released, a mafia spoof titled "The Gang That Couldn't Shoot Straight" came out featuring Jerry Orbach, who would later come to fame by playing Lenny Briscoe for several seasons on Law and Order and playing a character named Kid Sally Palumbo. Palumbo was partially based on Joe Gallo, and it was not a kind portrayal, showing him as a bumbling and incompetent mobster. Gallo confronted Orbach over the film, and they formed an odd friendship. Gallo had been with Orbach and his wife earlier that night, watching Don Rickles perform at the famous Copacabana Night Club

Gallo was a member of the Profaci Family, one of the five mafia families of New York City, which today is known as the Columbo Family. This was the youngest of the families, started by Joseph Profaci as his bootlegging gang grew in the late 20s. Gallo rose to become a capo in the Profaci gang, secretly owning several nightclubs and sweatshops as well as running gambling dens for the family. He and Carmine Persico took part in the murder of Albert Anastasia, head of the Anastasia family. Profaci ordered the hit, though likely at the behest of Carlo Gambino, Anastasia's underboss, who wanted to take control of the family. Gambino's gambit succeeded, and he took control of the American Mafia after the Appalachian Conference in 1957.

In the late 1950s, Gallo and his crew, which included his brothers and was known as the International Mob—as it included an Irishman, two Syrians, an Egyptian, a Puerto Rican, a Jew and a Greek—along with Carmine Persico's crew, found themselves fed up with their take of the Profaci family's profits. They devised a plan to take the top leadership of the Profaci family hostage to negotiate better terms. They succeeded in capturing four of Profaci's capos, including his brother, but Profaci was able to flee to safety in Florida. After several weeks of negotiation, Profaci agreed to their demands, and they released the hostages.

Profaci had no intention of following through with their demands, however, and quickly moved against them. He bribed Persico with a larger share of the family's rackets to switch sides. Persico set up a meeting with Joe Gallo's brother Larry, where he attempted to strangle him with a garrote until a police officer walked by and stopped the murder. Larry Gallo refused to testify, and the charges were dropped. Profaci ordered the murder of Joseph Gioielli, a member of Gallo's crew, and this hit was successful.

Due to the war, the Gallo crew spent the better part of a year held up in their hideout. This made them unable to handle the rackets that were the source of their illegal income, and they soon found themselves low on funds. Joe Gallo tried to extort a local cafe owner for protection money, a common mafia extortion racket where the criminals cause property damage to a store or restaurant if they do not pay for protection. The store owner reported Gallo to the police, and he was eventually sent to prison.

The war raged for another year after Joe Gallo was sent to prison. The Gallo crew bombed Persico's car, injuring but not killing him. They attempted to perform another hit on him, this time pulling up in a panel van and shooting him multiple times in the face, shoulder, and arm. Mafia legend holds that Persico spat out the bullet that hit his face after the attempted murder. Profaci died and was succeeded by Joseph Magliocco, though Magliocco's reign as the boss would be brief.

Magliocco and Joseph Bonanno, the head of the Bonanno Crime Family, devised a plot to take over the Mafia Commission. This plan included the murder of fellow New York City Bosses Carlo Gambino and Tommy Lucchese; Frank DeSimone, the head of the Los Angeles Crime Family; and Stefano Magaddino, the leader of the Buffalo Crime Family-centered in Western New York. Magliocco gave the contract to Joseph Colombo, who was one of the Profaci capos the Gallo's had kidnapped. Columbo did not attempt to kill the bosses, taking the information about the plot to the Mafia Commission instead, seeing an opportunity to take over the family himself. The Commission investigated the situation and according to their rules, called a mafia trial.

Bonanno chose to flee instead of submitting to the trial. Magliocco appeared and confessed to the plot. He was forced to retire from the Mafia and fined forty-three thousand dollars.

Columba was given the leadership position of the Profaci family, now named the Columbo Family, becoming both the youngest at 41, and the first American-born family head. The Gallo crew, now led by Larry Gallo since Joe Gallo was in prison, came to a peace settlement with Columbo, ending the war that had started two bosses ago. Larry Gallo passed away before his brother Joe was released from prison.

When Joe obtained his release from prison in 1971, Columbo came to him with an offer of one thousand dollars as a homecoming gift as well as a way to prevent further problems like the earlier war his crew had started. Joe Gallo refused the offer and demanded one hundred thousand dollars. To Joe Gallo, as he was in prison when his brother accepted the peace, it did not apply to him. Both Gallo and Columbo came away from the meeting, intending to have the other killed.

By this point, Joe Gallo was not Columbo's only enemy. He had been making waves in the Mafia community, bringing unwanted attention to their criminal enterprises. He created the Italian-American Civil Rights League with the purpose of protecting the Italian-American community from negative stereotypes that were common in pop culture. This group grew out of the previous Italian-American Anti-Defamation League that he created as an Astroturf protest organization in an attempt to show that his son's arrest related to a scheme to melt down silver dollars into ingots was due to bias against Italian-Americans.

The Italian-American Civil Rights League held an inaugural rally in New York City and put on a benefit concert headed by Frank Sinatra. When Francis Ford Coppola started making the first Godfather film, the production company worked with Columbo's Italian-American Civil Rights League to ensure that the film was not offensive to Italian-Americans. They reportedly removed any use of the word "Mafia" as well as "Cosa Nostra" from the film.

At the second Italian Unity Day rally put on by the Italian-American Civil Rights League, Jerome Johnson, an African American man with ties to the African-American gangs that controlled much of the crime in Harlem, obtained press credentials and gunned down Columbo as he was getting ready to speak at the rally. Columbo's security quickly dispatched Johnson, and while Columbo survived the shooting, he remained in a coma for the rest of his life.

The official police report labeled Johnson a lone gunman, making him solely responsible for the hit, but inside the mafia, Gallo was the top suspect. As he went to prison during a mafia war, Gallo found little friendship with the other mafiosos inside the prison—or as the monsters call it, at school. With little help from his own people, Gallo gravitated towards some African-American prisoners, becoming quite close to them. He even sued one of the prisons he was in after he was subjected to harsh treatment for allowing an African-American inmate barber to cut his hair. Gallo had plans with some African-American gangsters he met in prison to work together when they were out. His closeness to African-American criminals, added to the fact that Columbo was gunned down by an African-American gangster, was enough to convict him in the minds of the other Mafia heads—that he, like Columbo, seemed to enjoy a level of celebrity gave them further reasons to take him out.

At the same time, Sheeran's life had become much more complicated. With Hoffa in prison, controlling the union became a great deal more difficult. Hoffa's hand-picked successor,

Frank Fitzsimmons, had moved away from some of Hoffa's changes that gave the president of the Union more power. Fitzsimmons started to give more power back to the regional and local Unions. Others in the local and regional unions tried to wrest control of those locals from Hoffa's inner circle, Sheeran included.

An incident that took place at the Teamsters' Philadelphia union hall devolved into a riot when three thousand union members backing two different sides converged. The opposing leader ended upshot, and the police eventually arrested Sheeran for directing the murder. He remained in prison for months, losing his union election, before he was able to post bail. The charges were eventually dropped, but Sheeran was on the watch list of the authorities, both local and federal.

He still did the work that needed to be done for his friend Russell Bufalino. In fact, Bufalino called him up soon after Columbo was gunned down. Bufalino instructed him to pick up his little friend, a gun for use in a hit, and to contact his driver John Francis, known as the Red Head, who was an Irish gangster who used to run with the Irish Republican Army with their attacks on the United Kingdom. Francis and Sheeran had worked together on several murders on behalf of Bufalino. Over a decade later, when Francis was dying, he confessed to driving Sheeran to 14 different hits, including this one. Francis informed Sheeran that their target was Joe Gallo.

They expected Joe Gallo to eat at Umberto's Clam House for his birthday. Even though Gallo likely knew that others were gunning for him, eating at a place like Umberto's would have been seen as safe. The Mafia rules at the time made hits at restaurants in the Little Italy neighborhood off-limits. These hits were too loud and brought too much attention to the Mafia. They were also bad for the tourist business. Umberto's had extra protection, as well. It was secretly owned by Matthew Matty the Horse Lianniello, a Genovese Capo who owned an extensive collection of the adult entertainment businesses that lined Times Square in the 60s and 70s. The general mafia rules held that mafia-owned businesses were out of bounds for killing.

The rules the mafia live by are based on power, however, so when those with the most power want to change or break the rules, they can get away with it. Gallo, with the hit on Columbo, had himself broken the rules by having the hit made in such a public setting. The surviving heads of the five families of New York wanted Gallo dead, and they could get away with breaking the rules.

Sheeran and Francis knew that civilians would likely be nearby and that Gallo would have a bodyguard. Not hitting civilians would require an accurate shooter, and the presence of a bodyguard meant that getting closer than ten to fifteen feet from Gallo would be deadly dangerous. Sheeran dressed as a truck driver would make it look like he was just a regular person entering the restaurant to use the restroom. Francis would drive around the block and stop to meet Sheeran as he fled the scene.

Sheeran walked into the restaurant and spotted his target. The presence of Gallo's young daughter caused him to hesitate momentarily, but he thought he could take Gallo out without hitting her or the other civilians. He shot Gallo's bodyguard, Pete "The Greek" Diapoulas, a member of Gallo's crew during his war with the Profaci Family, in the lower back once before turning his fire onto Gallo. For his part, Gallo overturned the heavy butcher block table and started moving towards an exit, drawing the fire away from his family. He took bullets in the arm, back, and buttocks before collapsing on the sidewalk outside.

Sheeran walked out and got into the car, driven by Francis. After driving around long enough to make sure they were not tailed, including switching cars, Sheeran gave the gun to Francis, who took it apart and threw it in the river.

Witness accounts of the hit tell a different story. According to accounts from the scene, there were multiple gunmen involved in the hit. Sheeran contended that they were either mistaken, that eyewitness accounts in a stressful situation like a shooting can be erroneous, or that the witnesses intentionally lied. Friends and family of Gallo might not have wanted to admit that a lone gunman could pull off a hit on him.

The exact truth might never be known, and regardless of the veracity of Sheeran's claims, his life was about to take another turn after Gallo's death. Jimmy Hoffa was about to be pardoned, and he would look to Frank Sheeran to help him rebuild his fallen empire.

# Chapter 7: The Murder of Jimmy Hoffa

JIMMY HOFFA BEAT A string of charges pushed on him in the late 50s through the early 60s by Bobby Kennedy, first when he headed the McClellan Commission hearings over corruption in labor unions and organized crime and continuing Kennedy's brother Bobby as Attorney General after winning the 1960 presidential elections. They despised each other, and Bobby's determination to put Hoffa in prison only increased with every failure he suffered at Hoffa's hand. According to Sheeran, Hoffa aided in the assassination of President Kennedy in an attempt to push Bobby out as Attorney General, but Bobby Kennedy and the incoming president Johnson was able to put aside their differences. Bobby kept the attorney general job after his brother's death and continued his crusade against Hoffa.

He finally succeeded in convicting Hoffa on jury tampering charges related to a misdemeanor charge about a dummy corporation Hoffa had started in his wife's name. After three years of appeals, Hoffa finally went to prison in 1967, sentenced to an 8-year stretch. By this point, Bobby Kennedy had returned to the Senate and was contemplating a presidential run in 1968. An assassin's bullet ended his presidential aspirations, and in that way, gave Hoffa a chance at an early release from prison. That said, there was no connection between Bobby Kennedy's assassin, Sirhan Sirhan, and Hoffa. Bobby's death was just a lucky break for Hoffa; though, given Hoffa's post-prison years, he might have been safer in prison.

The winner of the 1968 presidential election was Richard Nixon. Nixon had run for president in 1960 after serving as Dwight Eisenhower's vice president for eight years. He lost that election to John Kennedy in one of the closest presidential elections in history, likely with Mafia help in Chicago. Given his history with Bobby Kennedy, Hoffa pushed the Teamsters to support Nixon in 1960. It was the only labor union to support the Republican presidential candidate.

Nixon was a brilliant man, but he was also wracked with paranoia. In his famous Checkers speech, after allegations of improper use of campaign funds when he was initially put on Eisenhower's ticket for the 1952 presidential election, Nixon said, "I've earned everything I've spent." This was more than true at the time. Nixon was born to parents of little means in Wittier, California. He went to the local college and joined the Navy prior to WWII. Sent to a logistic office, he repeatedly tried to get a combat position to do more for the war. After the war, he made it to Congress and then to the Senate through his work ethic and sheer determination. He lived the American Dream.

In 1960, he faced an opponent in the form of John Kennedy, who had a very similar resume with a wartime stint in the Navy, followed by Congress and then the Senate. The main difference was in how Kennedy achieved these things. When Nixon was stuck in a logistics office begging to get into combat, Joe Kennedy, Kennedy's rich father, talked to a few men in the war department and got his son a position in Naval intelligence after John had failed his physical. When John Kennedy returned and wanted to run for Congress, Joe Kennedy talked to the current officeholder, and he decided not to run for reelection. When Kennedy went for the Senate, his father offered the biggest paper in Massachusetts an interest-free loan before they endorsed his son for the Office. Nixon's loss in 1960 fed his paranoia. He had worked his entire life, gotten everything he had, and lost to someone who had the right family. Nixon was always willing to do whatever it took to win, but now he'd go even further.

President Nixon came into the 1972 election as a popular incumbent. While he had not ended the Vietnam war, he had opened relations with China. All of the polls showed him well ahead of the Democratic nominee, George McGovern. This was not enough for Nixon. Paranoid of the Democrats and internal leaks to the press, he formed a group called the White House Plumbers as part of his reelection to ferret out the leaks. The plumbers went much further, performing several burglaries of democratic offices or places associated with top Democrats in searches for more dirt. The most famous of these was in the Watergate Hotel, where the burglars were caught. This would eventually lead to the Watergate scandal and cover-up that would finish with Nixon resigning from office. The irony of these actions was that Nixon won in a historic landslide, winning 520 electoral votes and carrying 49 states. Nixon's team never had to do any of the things that led to his resignation in order to win.

Even though he was in prison, Hoffa was a popular figure in the union. As he supported Nixon in '60, Nixon's people approached Hoffa in '71, offering a commutation of his sentence for the support of the Teamsters. Hoffa agreed and was released from prison, while the Teamsters endorsed Nixon in '72. Not part of the agreement was the condition that Hoffa was not to get involved in union leadership until 1980. Hoffa sued to remove the condition but lost the battle in court.

While Hoffa was in prison, he had given the presidency to Frank Fitzsimmons. Instead of running the union as Hoffa had, Fitzsimmons started to work at decentralizing the union power, returning some to the regional offices and the locals themselves. Regarding dealings with the Mafia, Fitzsimmons was much more amicable to deals favorable to the mafia figures than Hoffa was. Hoffa always took control and made sure that he got a sizable cut of any illegal proceeds. Despite his ban from leadership, Hoffa became obsessed with taking back the union from Fitzsimmons, going so far as even to plot Fitzsimmons' murder.

After a few more years out of prison, his obsession grew, and he began talking dangerously. He had records and information on all of the underworld figures that he had dealt with as president of the Teamsters. He began talking about releasing that information if he did not get control of the union. He even started to claim that he would make sure to push the mafia out of the unions if he became president again.

This was a popular idea in the mid-70s. The Watergate scandal had shown Americans that there was corruption at the highest level of the government, and the mafia's place in the criminal world was in the spotlight as never before. *The Godfather* had been released in 1972 and became a multi-Academy Award-winning blockbuster and showed the Mafia in a way that had never been done before. The Mafia was on the mind of a lot of people.

The biggest blow to Hoffa in the mind of the leaders of the American Mafia was his promise to reign in the use of the Teamster's pension fund to loan out to mafia operations. Loans from the pension fund had built the casinos in Havana and Las Vegas as well as a multitude of other major Mafia projects. The Mafia could not use regular banks to finance their building projects without laundering their money. Losing access to the pension fund was unacceptable to them. Fitzsimmons had the vote of the Mafia when it came to the Teamster's presidency.

Hoffa just did not listen and became increasingly unhinged as 1975 approached. He often talked about himself in the third person, and while he had always been a man who could be quick to anger, he started to be taken with fits of irrational anger. Hoffa had been having issues with a Capo of the Genovese Crime Family named Anthony Tony Pro Provenzano. They had both been in the same prison for a while and had started as allies, with Hoffa supporting Tony Pro's attempt to control a Teamster local in New Jersey. Their relationship soured, and Tony Pro was adamant in keeping Hoffa out of the leadership. Frank Sheeran, with his connections in both the Teamsters and the Mafia, through Russell Bufalino, repeatedly tried to keep the peace, but Hoffa wouldn't listen to his old friend.

In the summer of 1975, the daughter of Bill Bufalino, no relation to Russell Bufalino, was scheduled to happen in Detroit. Bill Bufalino was the main lawyer for the Teamsters and had extensive ties to the Mafia. Like the wedding in *The Godfather*, it would be a well-attended event among mafiosos. Sheeran was going to be driving Russell Bufalino to the wedding. Hoffa was skipping the wedding due to his deteriorating position among the mafia. Sheeran had asked Bufalino for one last chance to try and get Hoffa to back away from his plans to take back the union.

Sheeran called Hoffa a few days before the wedding, but Hoffa still wouldn't listen. Hoffa claimed to be untouchable because if he died, all the information he had on the mob would be released. Sheeran brought up Sam Momo Giancana, the boss of the Chicago Outfit. Giancana had been killed the month before. News had recently broken about Giancana and Bufalino's connections with the CIA in the CIA's attempts on Castro's life and with the Bay of Pigs invasion. The United States Congress had set up hearings on the issue and subpoenas Giancana. The week before, Giancana's body was found in the kitchen of his home with one bullet shot into the back of his head, and five others shot into his face. It was speculated that Giancana knew and was friendly with his murderer, as he had been cooking sausage and peppers at the time. Giancana had a heart issue and could not eat that type of food.

Sheeran argued that if Giancana was not untouchable, neither was Hoffa. Hoffa claimed that his records made him different. Giancana never wrote anything down. Killing him killed everything he knew and did. In the end, all Sheeran could do was to get Hoffa to agree to meet with himself and Bufalino when they reached Detroit. The next day, Hoffa called Sheeran and told him that the Detroit boss, Antony Tony Jack Giacalone, had agreed to hold a meeting between Hoffa and Tony Pro to be held at the Machus Red Fox Restaurant in Detroit. To Sheeran, this seemed like a reasonable place for such a meeting and agreed to join Hoffa in the Meeting.

On their drive to Detroit with their wives, Sheeran and Bufalino made several stops, leaving the wives at a coffee shop, while the men went on errands for Bufalino, picking up money or leaving instructions to members of his crime family. While away from their wives, Bufalino informed Sheeran that they would be getting to Detroit after Hoffa's meeting. Bufalino did not want Sheeran by Hoffa's side in the meeting, and Sheeran knew enough to understand why.

Hoffa was marked for death and would never leave that meeting. If Sheeran were there, he would be killed too. Everyone in the Mafia knew Sheeran was close to Hoffa, and it was only through Bufalino's intervention that Sheeran himself was not marked for death, either. Sheeran tried one last time to save Hoffa's life with no success. The next day, Bufalino ordered Sheeran to take a quick flight to Detroit and to perform the hit himself. Sheeran's presence would keep the sometimes irrational Hoffa calm, and it was Sheeran's chance to show his true loyalty. Sheeran understood that Bufalino was offering him a choice: kill Hoffa or be killed himself. Either way, Hoffa's days were numbered. Sheeran made his way to the airport.

After a quick flight across Lake Erie, Sheeran got into the car left for him and made his way to the house Hoffa would die in. There he met Tony Pro's man Sally Bugs, as well as Hoffa's foster son Chucky O'Brien. They loaded into the car Chucky was driving, owned by Giacalone, and made their way to the restaurant where Hoffa was supposed to meet Giacalone and Tony Pro. Neither of them made the meeting. Both made sure to be out of town while the deed was done.

Hoffa was agitated when they arrived because of the missed meetings, but Sheeran told him that he was taking him to meet Bufalino. Bufalino was a cautious man and wouldn't meet in a restaurant he didn't know, so this was not a strange request. After they reached the house, O'Brien and Sally Bugs drove off while Hoffa entered the house before Sheeran. Realizing the house was empty, not knowing the cleanup crew was in the back, Hoffa realized that his time was up.

Hoffa pushed past Sheeran, reaching for the door. Sheeran assumed that Hoffa thought Sheeran was still his man and that they both were targets. He never knew that he was wrong. Sheeran shot Hoffa twice in the back of the head.

Once Hoffa fell, Sheeran waited for a few moments. He knew Bufalino had his back, and while Bufalino was a powerful figure in the Mafia, he was not at the top of the snake. Sheeran worried that his connection to Hoffa could lead to him being killed as well. When nothing happened, he dropped the gun, walked out of the house, and drove the car back to the airport. Less than an hour later, he and Bufalino picked up their wives and continued their trip to Detroit for the wedding.

After Sheeran's confession, investigation combed the house where he claimed that Hoffa was killed. They found old bloodstains where Sheeran indicated they would, but they were too old to be conclusively analyzed. Jimmy Hoffa was never seen again.

# Conclusion

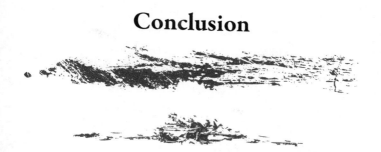

WITH HOFFA GONE, THE Teamster's union fell on harder times. It fractured some, as different factions attempted to take control while President Fitzsimmons worked to decentralize its structure, returning power back to the regional and local offices. The Federal Government's deregulation of the freight industry in 1980 further crippled the union's power.

For Frank Sheeran, the years after Hoffa were fraught with legal challenges. His less-than-legal work within the union had already caught the attention of law enforcement, and as the 70s came to a close, both state and federal authorities were closing in. He was able to beat several charges, earning acquittals, but they eventually charged him with something he could not beat because they caught him on a wire.

Sheeran had been recorded instructing one of his men to break the legs of the manager of a crane company in retaliation for firing some of Sheeran's men. Worse for Sheeran, he had been caught by the FBI picking up dynamite from an arms company owned by Bufalino that he intended to use to blow up the office of the crane company. He was convicted on both counts and sent to jail.

His old friend Russell Bufalino found himself in prison at the same time. He had tried to have a witness killed before his trial but hired a government informant to do the deed. For a while, he and Sheeran reunited in prison. Bufalino was released and died at the age of 90. He maintained some control over his mafia family to the end, though watched by the FBI.

Sheeran got a medical release from prison, and the FBI hounded him as well, looking for anything to send him back. They found it when he was caught socializing with John Stanfa, the boss of the Philadelphia Mafia at the time, the fourth boss the Philly Family had after Sheeran's friend Angelo Bruno was gunned down in 1980.

Sheeran returned to prison for 10 months at the age of 75. During his time in prison, the FBI repeatedly tried to get him to confess to further crimes and to turn rat on the Mafia. He never did, holding his story till his deathbed when almost all of the mafia members he worked for and with had already passed. Sheeran died on December 14, 2003, in a Philadelphia nursing home at the age of 83.

THANK YOU FOR MAKING it through to the end of *The Irishman: Frank Sheeran's True Crime Story*, let's hope it was informative and able to provide you with an insight into the life and times of Frank Sheeran, The Irishman.

Finally, if you found this book useful in any way, a review is always appreciated!

# Don't miss out!

Visit the website below and you can sign up to receive emails whenever Daniel Brand publishes a new book. There's no charge and no obligation.

https://books2read.com/r/B-A-YKHF-BWKV

Connecting independent readers to independent writers.

Did you love *The Irishman: Frank Sheeran's The True Crime Story*? Then you should read *How To Think Like A Spy: Spy Secrets and Survival Techniques That Can Save You and Your Family*[1] by Daniel Brand!

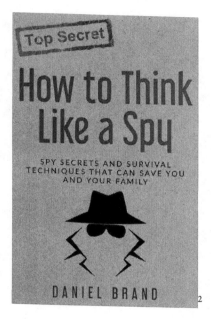

[2]

Do you often dream of becoming a top-secret operative? Do the televisions shows such as *The Americans* or *The Bourne Identity* catch your attention? Do you find yourself highly engaged in articles about new and improved spy gadgets? Are you curious about what spy skills it really takes to be undercover and work as an emissary? If that's the case, you have stumbled across a one-of-a-kind book that discusses the valuable and applicable spy secrets

1. https://books2read.com/u/bWZYlG

2. https://books2read.com/u/bWZYlG

about the mental and physical aspects one must possess in order to become a spy!

**The contents of this book include:**

*Tips of getting into the mindset that is needed to survive dangerous scenarios*

*Situational awareness skills that can help you de-escalate situations*

*How to secure your home to protect yourself and your family*

*Safety skills needed when traveling*

*Methods of deciphering when someone is being dishonest*

*Self-defense skills that can be utilized in a variety of situations*

*Skills to help you disappear without a trace*

*Driving skills that will come in handy in the case you need to get away quickly*

*Surveillance skills necessary to survey detailed situations*

If you are unsure you have what it takes to become your own version of a master undercover operative, then the chapters in this book will not only help you build up the confidence you need in yourself, but it will also assist in looking at yourself as a person in a different light! We all have special skill sets, so why not learn how to put them to good use as you learn to mold your mind into that of a spy?

**How To Think Like Spy** was created to be a fun, easy-to-read, and entertaining source of useful information that could help readers really sink their teeth into the behind the scenes life of a spy. I hope you find it resourceful in the case you need to evade danger or seek personal intel on people in your life.

Made in the USA
San Bernardino, CA
01 February 2020

63879882R00051